A Soldier's Story

Strength Despite Adversity

By

Tomika Prouty

A Soldier's Story

Strength Despite Adversity

Table of Contents

Straight Outta Macon

I came "Straight Outta Macon" from an impoverished neighborhood called Unionville; a place known for its' drug dealers who were literally on every corner and felt a sense of entitlement, freely encamping themselves in my neighborhood, around my sanctuary I called home. Growing up in the "hood" wasn't a passport to bad behavior. My mom taught us early, we were in the environment, but the environment was not a part of us.

My sanctuary included living with my mom, grandparents, great grand-mom, three siblings, two uncles and an aunt. My mom and maternal elders made sure we knew about Jesus Christ at an early age. We attended Sunday School, Church, Vacation Bible School, Revivals and participated in community marches. I vividly remember marching the streets of

Unionville carrying lighted candles with my church, pleading with the drug dealers to leave the neighborhood and give their lives to God. My inner sanctuary was a single room shared with my siblings and our mom. I am forever grateful for my humble beginnings and early introduction to my Lord and Savior.

My mom met the love of her life, Christopher, in 1981 and they were married at my childhood church, Center Hill Baptist Church in Macon, Georgia. I was young when my mom and dad married, and Christopher never carried the title of a stepfather. The term never applied to him because he never conducted himself as such or the way I thought a stepfather would act. You could not tell him we were not his girls. This was new and refreshing, not that I experienced anything negative prior, but I often forgot he wasn't my biological father. He worked for the government and after they were married, we moved to Texas. The move provided us with a different lifestyle than afforded to us in Macon. We instantly went from low-income to middle class. Unfortunately, my mom became homesick, as this was her first time away from family and the marriage ended in divorce shortly thereafter.

We returned to Macon, the same neighborhood in Unionville. My mom did her absolute best to make sure we were safe, clean, and properly nurtured. Thank God for family; helping my mom take care of us. I was always the leader among my siblings. I took charge at home and helped my mom with my siblings. I did not have to, nor was I forced because my mom did a great job taking care of us, but I had a "take charge" attitude even at an early age. The one tragedy I'll never forget during this time of my life is the passing of my grandmother Rosa. I was 15 years old. She asked to be taken to the hospital where she passed away about a week later. That was one of the worse moments of my life. Our family was devastated. My grandmother loved us unconditionally. I remember, it snowed one winter, and she walked less than a mile to my aunt and uncle's home to take them breakfast. That was the kind of woman she was.

My senior year of high school, we were told recruiters were coming to administer the Armed

Services Vocational Aptitude Battery (ASVAB). I had absolutely no desire to join the military at this time, however, God has a way of changing plans, and I signed up to take the test. When graduation approached, I knew I could not remain in Macon. I had to escape!

I was scared I wouldn't be there for my mom to help with my sisters, as I have done for as long as I could remember. Nevertheless, I was excited about ways I could support them financially and yet fulfill my dreams of being someone "great." One day, after much thought and conversation with my dad, I decided to join the Army Reserve to give me the best of both worlds; being there for my family and creating a life of my own. As I prepared to leave my family for a short period of time for training, my cousin braided my hair in micro braids. This single act of my beloved cousin meant I had one less thing to worry about, as I started this chapter of my life.

In The Army Now

I went to Basic Training at Fort Jackson, South Carolina in the winter of 1993, having no idea what to expect. When I arrived, I asked myself, "What did you get yourself into?" I remember my Drill Sergeant looked at my hair and started screaming. You guessed it! I had to take the micro braids out. I had a matter of hours to do so. My battle buddies came to my rescue; mission accomplished. That was my first real experience of (camaraderie) setting the stage for the rest of my military career.

After months of hardcore training, I was not prepared for the transition back into the relaxed environment I left. Neither was I prepared to return and not find employment. I worked at a restaurant and became a Team Leader instantly because of my military training and willingness to step up. Shortly after returning home, Macon had one of the worse flood disasters ever. The flood of 94' activated my Reserve unit to provide the citizens with water, as the local water supply wasn't safe to drink. It is one event I'll never forget. You knew it was bad when the infamous Ocmulgee River overflowed. We were in disbelief. I never experienced anything of that magnitude in my life. Homes and businesses were severely damaged or destroyed, bridges collapsed, and caskets uprooted and began to float.

My family members came to retrieve water. The look on their faces seeing me in uniform, serving the citizens was one of absolute joy and pride. My family could not be prouder of the woman I had become at such a tender age of eighteen. That was a highlight for me. After six months, I decided the Army Reserve and restaurant life was not for me. I needed more of a challenge as well as an increase in finances. I called the recruiter who assisted me with my enlistment in the Army Reserve and discussed enlisting in the Active Army. There my real journey began.

The first stop on my new life's journey was Fort Hood, Texas. Fort Hood introduced me to the "real"

Army and quite frankly…life. I grew up fast! I was now nineteen years old, married and pregnant. My highlight was being assigned to positions of trust with senior leaders. I'll never forget the Command Sergeant Major (CSM), CSM Jones. He believed in me at such a young age and told me he was going to place me in a position to go far in the Army (he was a vessel being used by God) and he was right (by the grace of God); I excelled. I remember being extremely shy, at 5 feet 2 inches and ninety-five pounds! My CSM said he was going to help me overcome my shyness. Each morning I had to walk to the Company from Headquarters where I was assigned, to tell the First Sergeant (1SG), good morning. I was petrified. During that time, mid 90's, you did not report to the 1SG unless you were in trouble. As each day passed, I gained more and more confidence. Mission accomplished! I'll never forget this assignment because my life had changed so much. It was also a time where the world around me had changed dramatically too. It is here, I learned of O.J. Simpson being charged, tried and acquitted of Nicole Simpson's and Ron Goldman's death. It was the first time TV cameras were allowed in a courtroom and a celebrity assembled dream team, unlike anything the world had ever seen. As a young Private with a family, I was not making a lot of money and jobs were scarce in Killeen. I remember vividly, my Master Sergeant (MSG) called me into the office with the CSM and Colonel (COL) to tell me life was too hard for us there and they had an assignment that would be great financially for me and my husband (ex-husband now). I wasn't ready to leave Texas as I wasn't used to changes at that time but after praying and talking to my dad (Christopher, remember him), mom and cousin who were also stationed there, I accepted the assignment. I received a PERSGRAM (Personnel Telegram) or assignment instructions and off to the District of Columbia we went!

Defense Intelligence Agency, Bolling Air Force Base - As I previously stated, I was petrified of moving to D.C., I wasn't ready. Once again, I found myself working in a position of trust. As a Private First Class (PFC), I had the enormous responsibility of a newsletter that was read by the Commander in Chief, President of the United States, talk about weight on me! However, I was groomed throughout my previous duty station, therefore, I accepted the pressure of this position. Three years passed, I was now preparing to re-enlist or receive an honorable discharge.

There's no way I could be discharged, I loved the Army and decided to re-enlist for another three years! I remember my supervisor asking where I'd like to have my ceremony and I jokingly said, "The White House" and went on about the day. One night I received a phone call from my supervisor and he said, "Tell your family to wear comfortable shoes tomorrow for your ceremony." I totally forgot I said the White House and low and behold we were walking to the Metro. I re-enlisted right outside the President's bedroom window (so I was told). That was definitely a highlight for my family. Now it's time to move again.

Miami, Florida – My assignment at Defense Intelligence Agency had come to an end and I prepared to move to Miami, Florida for an assignment at United States Southern Command. I enjoyed all my assignments for different reasons. Here it was the weather and great leadership, I will never forget my supervisor, Master Sergeant (MSG) McClymont. He allowed me to make mistakes without fear of getting into trouble and there I learned a great deal. I had an enormous amount of confidence now with almost five years in the Army, thanks to my former CSM.

My highlight was an Opa Locka police officer who spent ten years trying to receive a medal that was rightfully his. When I came on board, I took matters into my own hands, called the Army Human Resources Command and within hours I had this officer's award. No one could believe what took ten years for others took hours for me. I received numerous accolades, even from an Army two-star general and a Marine Corps one-star general. I was one proud Soldier!

Endings and Beginnings

After six years of marriage, I filed for and was granted a divorce; where I remained in this status for ten years. In the midst of all the great things that happened during this assignment, one horrific day occurred, 9/11. I remember sitting in my cubicle at work when I received a phone call from my ex-husband asking me was I watching the news and proceeded to explain what was happening. That was one of the worse days of my life. Everyone was scrambling at work and no work got done for the remainder of the day, nor the days to follow. Everyone was calling their family and friends in the D.C. area, who worked at the Pentagon. Remember my supervisor, MSG McClymont, he was at the Pentagon for a meeting! Thank God he was out of harm's way and arrived back safely to Miami. We were ready for war! Fast-forward, I was promoted to Sergeant and attended the Staff Sergeant Board. Unfortunately, my time in Miami came to an end and it was time to move to Hawaii.

Honolulu, Hawaii - United States Pacific Command – I arrived in Hawaii from Miami in September. There wasn't much of a change in weather. I adjusted well. As soon as I arrived I started college the following month. I have always been fascinated with law and enjoyed watching shows like Law and Order, Cops and America's Most Wanted. It was befitting to study Justice Administration. I completed all requirements and was awarded an Associate of Arts in Justice Administration from Hawaii Pacific University and started on my B.A. degree. I was a member of the Honor Cordon and Color Guard. We participated in numerous events around the Island. My highlight was getting promoted to Staff Sergeant (SSG) when a lot of people thought it was impossible because of the transformation the Army was going through. The Army was deleting my Military Occupational Specialty (MOS). My MOS had a low rate of promotion as the scores stayed maxed out, meaning you would have to get an astronomical amount of points to be promoted. You literally had to achieve the max in every area such as Physical Training,

Education, and Weapons, to name a few. It was not easy but as a single mom I could not afford and did not want to change jobs because of the uncertainty. I always said, I'm a Soldier but I am a mother first. A lot of people did not grasp that. You can have both with balance. I made it work. It was a struggle getting promoted (faster) for that reason but I never regretted it. As time passed, I was promoted to SSG! Many were surprised as previously stated, but I wasn't because I serve an awesome God. He knew my heart and blessed me accordingly.

Fast-forward; by this point I had been in Hawaii six years when I received a phone call that my great grandmom was sick. I talked to her and asked her to hold on. I told her I would be home in about ten days as I was finally moving from Hawaii back to the Mainland. She told me okay, but God had another plan. She passed away and I could not get home as I was in the middle of transitioning from Hawaii. I was hurt but I knew she was in a better place. After seven long years, we were still at war and my time finally came to answer the call. It was time to trade in the sunny weather for rugged terrain and combat gear. Afghanistan here I come!

However, I had to get to Fort Campbell first.

Ft. Campbell, Kentucky, home of the 101st Airborne (Screaming Eagles). My son was not able to move to Kentucky with me because of my pending deployment. I trained for approximately forty-five days. This was my first and only deployment. I was anxious to go to war yet nervous to leave my family, especially my son. I was going to a place I'd never been, with people I did not know (as I had only been with my new unit about forty-five days) under less than desirable conditions. I did not know what to expect and quite frankly, although I am a believer, I had thoughts of not returning home. I have faith, yet I knew the reality of war. My anxiety started kicking in and I became sad, frustrated and even angry. As I sat in briefings as to why we must go, the anger, sadness, and frustration turned to excitement. Yes, I know, weird! I was ready to go to war! Even if I wasn't, I had no choice. While I was preparing for war, I was also preparing my military records for the Sergeant First Class (SFC) selection board. I was told by my peers I would not be selected to SFC on my first look because I did not meet any of the prerequisites, as well as the promotion rate on your first look, is almost impossible for my MOS. I did not listen. I completed all the paperwork, submitted it and waited for the results. BREAKING NEWS: Barack Obama won the Presidential election! He is now the 44th President of the United States. My great-grandmother passed away two months earlier. Listening to her sharing stories during my childhood, I know she never thought this moment would ever be possible; a man of color in the White House. An unprecedented event (my thoughts in that moment)! Now back to business, I enlisted into the military to serve, protect and defend our Country. Wheels up!

Deployment to Afghanistan – I'm here! I could not believe I arrived in Afghanistan two days prior to Christmas. The weather was nice in the location I was assigned. It reminded me of my assignments in Miami and Hawaii. As we settled in, I started becoming anxious, nervous and scared again. I began to pray and ask God to see us through this deployment and protect us from our enemy. The bay I lived in was small and dreary. My roommates were pilots with weird hours, which caused me and my Battle Buddy to walk and talk quietly. It was nerve wrecking because I had to stand outside late at night to talk on the phone to my family and friends back in the United States. It was pitch black when I walked to the latrine, the shower area and from work after my shift ended. I didn't know if I was going to be attacked or worse, killed. I would rush through my shower. I wanted to be back in my bay because I felt some sort of security from the outside element.

One day as my Battle Buddy Taylor and I were walking, a rocket propelled grenade (RPG) was fired into our forward operating base (FOB). All I heard was a loud and eerie sound and we scattered to safety. We were always on alert because you never knew when an attack would happen. Our makeshift gym was attacked as well as our dining facility. While our FOB was unsettling and constantly being attacked, so was my son. He was not doing well in his temporary environment. He was fighting his own battle at twelve years old. I was worried about him as well as myself. My dad was also fighting a battle and would later succumb to cancer. He tried to conceal his diagnosis when he found out a year earlier. I had orders to deploy to Afghanistan and he wanted me to focus on the mission and return home safely; not worried about him. Eventually, he broke down and told me. He did not want to pass away while I was deployed and not know he was diagnosed with cancer. As much as I love this Nation, I wanted to be home to protect my son and be there for my dad during the biggest battle of his life.

Prayer has always been a huge part of my life. I knew then as I know now, the power of prayer and there was no way I was going to let the enemy win. I had to make it home alive and well. The deployment was taking a toll on me mentally because I was worried about my family. After talking to my son one night, I literally fell to the ground, on my knees, and began to cry out to God. As I cried out in distress I saw a light, then immediately peace came upon me and my tears literally stopped. I knew in that moment that God had answered my prayer. I'm going back to Hawaii!

Previously, I told you about the criteria for promotion to Sergeant First Class and how people said I would not be promoted on this Board because I did not meet any of the prerequisites. The results were released while I was deployed. I made it! God promoted me, not man. The God I serve is faithful to His children. He proved to a lot of people who doubted me based off man's criteria for promotion to the senior ranks, Sergeant First Class (SFC). I was so excited, I screamed. I almost woke up the enemy.

That was truly one of my deployment highlights, as well as making a difference in Afghanistan. This is also the time when the news media were in a frenzy as word spread of Michael Jackson's death. The world was in disbelief. Moving forward, I must admit, returning home to my family was the ultimate highlight of my deployment. Redeploying was nearing and I was one of about six Staff Sergeants (promotable) who received a Meritorious Service Medal (MSM). That was exciting!

Redeployment – I was reunited with my son after ten long months! I missed him tremendously, as well as my mom, dad, siblings, family and friends. I had a hard time adjusting, though, as did he. I was still on high alert as my body had been programmed for almost a year. Every small noise scared me, every door closed scared me and every car that backfired had me running for cover. My attitude was different, and my patience was shorter. I knew there was a problem, but I was hesitant to talk to someone due to the high level of positions of trust I was assigned to throughout my career. I suppressed it and kept it moving. Besides, my son was my priority, not the issues I brought home with me. However, I cried out to God. He heard my cry and I was able to suppress what happened during the deployment; at least for the next five years. After talking to my chain of command, they understood the needs of my son and allowed me to request another assignment. I knew it was well because God said so as I cried out to Him in Afghanistan. We are going back to Hawaii, not to U.S. Pacific Command this time but to Joint POW/MIA Accounting Command (JPAC), now named Defense POW/MIA Accounting Agency.

JPAC (now named Defense POW/MIA Accounting Agency), Joint Base Pearl Harbor - Hickam, Hawaii – JPAC was another awesome assignment. I was the Senior Human Resources Sergeant. As soon as I arrived in Hawaii my grandfather passed away. I was devastated. I hurt for my mom because now her mom and dad were no longer here on earth. My son and I flew to Macon to attend his home going celebration. We returned to Hawaii two weeks later. Shortly thereafter, I received Orders as I had a temporary duty (TDY) in Thailand. My mom flew to Hawaii to care for my son in my absence. As a matter of fact, it was her first time flying and her first-time visiting Hawaii. I enjoyed Thailand despite the hot and muggy weather. My mom enjoyed Hawaii and when she returned to Macon, my son and I continued to bond and heal.

It was time to gain normalcy back into our lives. As God knows the desires of our heart, after some time went by, I meet a guy named Craig. We dated for a short period of time when he asked me to marry him. I accepted his proposal and gained three beautiful daughters. My mom, uncle, best friend, dad (my dad diagnosed with cancer) and his wife flew to Hawaii to be a part of our special day. It was awesome being with family during such a happy occasion. We had a beautiful yet intimate wedding in a private garden in

Honolulu and honeymoon in Maui.

After celebrating our nuptials with family and going on our honeymoon everyone returned home. It had been two days or so since I last spoke with my Dad, I called him, but his wife frantically told me she would call me back. I did not know he stopped breathing (the paramedics were on the scene) prior to me calling. When his wife returned my called, she gave me the news no child wants to hear. He gained his wings less than five months after walking me down the aisle. I truly believe he held on long enough to witness that moment and knew I would be in good hands marrying a man after God's own heart.

I was devastated, hurt, angry and lost. I will always be daddy's little girl. There were two homegoing celebrations for him simultaneously in two locations, Macon, Georgia and Texarkana, Texas. We flew to Macon to attend his home going and returned home ten days later. Our daughters came to visit us in Hawaii. They had a blast. We vacationed at the Alana Disney Resort & Spa, went shopping, and hung out at several beaches including the infamous Waikiki Beach. Their vacation finally came to an end and they returned to Minnesota.

It's graduation time, Wow! Where did the time go? My mom, uncle, and aunt were back in Hawaii to celebrate yet another milestone in our son's life. As this celebration came to an end our family departed the Island. I realized the long road we traveled and anticipating retirement had me nervous as the Army was my life. Quite frankly, it was all I knew. I was barely eighteen when I joined and had served almost twenty years by this point.

God Calls

I birthed House of Stone by CoCo, LLC – As I approached my 20th year, I contemplated what I wanted to do with "life after the Army." Joining the workforce wasn't an option at that time as I was still dealing with issues from my deployment to Afghanistan. Remember, my "issues" were suppressed for five years. All of a sudden, it all came crashing down at once; migraines, anxiety attacks, depression, neck, back and chest pain and blurred vision. I was embarrassed. I did not know how to process it, nor did I want to deal with it. After all, I now had to deal with the emotional and physical trauma my son was subjected to while I was deployed. I was angry.

Unfortunately, because I did not deal with the issues from my deployment, they resurfaced. This time there was no way to neither deny the issues nor continue to pretend everything was okay. I remember having anxiety attacks back to back. It initially started out once a week. As time progressed, it went from once a week to a few times a week to a couple times a day. I have always been a strong woman yet no matter how strong you are, you can only suppress issues for so long until it is time to deal with them. I continued to pray the Word of God and seek His face for help during this period of my life. I knew I could not work as I continued to deal with the effects of the deployment. I've always wanted to own my own business and already had an entrepreneurial spirit. I was a consultant for Mary Kay, Home Interior, Pre-Paid Legal and Thirty-One bags, all while serving on active duty. After speaking with my husband about my desire to start a business after I retire, he was on board and gave me his blessing. It was on now!

During this timeframe, after our son graduated from high school, I asked him to design a t-shirt so I can promote it but he wasn't interested. I wanted him to have an option if college or a 9 to 5 didn't work out. The idea stayed with me, as I did not see a lot of t-shirts in Hawaii that displayed positive messages. Before long, my Turn't Up 4 JESUS T-shirt was birthed. It sold extremely well and still sells today. Although I was still fighting through the issues of deployment, my faith, family and running my business kept me going. Despite my experience in Afghanistan, my faith and family would not let me stay in a state of anxiety or depression. 1 Thessalonians 5:17 (NKJV) *"Pray without ceasing."* I am always in constant communion with God and P-U-S-H (Pray Until Something Happens) myself daily to persevere through it all. I have too much to live for to be held captive from my experience in Afghanistan. Our time in Hawaii came to an end and I started having second thoughts about retiring. Yes, even as a believer, I was nervous. I didn't say I doubted God wouldn't come through. I knew God would take care of us, yet I decided to give the Army one more tour. After almost twenty years it was hard to walk away from the Army. Goodbye, Hawaii!

We arrived at Fort Stewart, Georgia. After being here for a short period, I decided to submit my request for retirement. I quickly realized some personnel in leadership positions accepted the blatant disrespect that junior Soldiers displayed towards Senior leadership. After nearly twenty-one years in the Army, it was time to hang up the uniform. During this time, I was still dealing with the effects of Afghanistan. Needless to say, dealing with disrespectful Soldiers, didn't help my anger issues and anxiety.

Retirement just felt right. All I wanted was to feel normal again, the way I felt before I deployed. I was exhausted from constantly going to the emergency room for anxiety attacks. I was sick and tired of being sick and tired. One night while my husband was deployed I started having an anxiety attack, I was scared but I had enough. I refused to give him (the enemy) my life. I was ready to fight. I laid prostrate on a black rug in my family room and cried out to God. I cried, prayed and cried some more, like never before. My husband kept me lifted in prayer even from afar. I knew God wanted to hear my cry and I cried out! I laid hands on myself. When I got up, my throat was sore from crying out, but God answered my prayer. His miraculous power had consumed me and healed me from anxiety attacks.

Depression continued. The enemy's only plan was

to lead me to a life of destruction with depression, But God! After years of prayer for healing from depression I finally fought the enemy back the way I should have all alone. I thought I was fighting him, but in reality, I allowed him to fight me.

I had nightmares from deployment, dark vivid dreams would appear, I thought I was going crazy. I was hesitant to talk to other believers, as some are judgmental, insensitive, arrogant, and unfortunately, have forgotten the battles they fought before Christ healed them. I had ladies in the Church tell me, "you are not praying hard enough," or asking, "is your husband praying for you?" They often rationalized their insensitivity by saying depression is not of God. They were absolutely correct (however, delivery is important in Ministry), 2 Timothy 1:7 (KJV) states, *"For God hath not given us the spirit of fear; but of power, and of love, and of a sound mind."* I knew God's Will was not for me to battle depression and that everything happens for a reason but in the end, God will get the Glory. Because I bared the burden of anxiety and depression among other issues, I knew it would help me witness to the hurt, lost and unsaved. I didn't understand it while walking through the fire, but I quickly realized the depth of Romans 8:28 (KJV) *"And we know that all things work together for good to those who love God, to those who are the called according to His purpose."*

People don't want to hear what you learned in college they want to hear a testimony. They want to hear how you went through the fire and came out unscathed. They want to connect with you; they want to know you truly understand their testimony. We must be obedient to God even in our wilderness. There's always a lesson to be learned. Colossians 3:2 (NKJV) states *"set your mind on things above…"*! Several other scriptures came to mind, Jeremiah 29:11 (KJV) *"For I know the thoughts that I think towards you, saith the LORD, thoughts of peace, and not of evil, to give you an expected end."* Isaiah 54:17 (NKJV), *"No weapon that is formed against thee shall prosper…,"* I believe God allowed me to go through a season of depression so I would have a testimony to help others who are struggling because of a lack of sensitivity in the Church. Somewhere in that season of my life, I began to feel inadequate, I felt misunderstood, I did not feel validated, and I always wondered why I never fit in. There were many lies going through my mind from the enemy. As I began to form a more intimate relationship with God He began to heal me. Years later, I no longer feel the need to be validated by others. I don't mind being unique and not fitting in. I don't feed into inadequacy. Through fervent prayer and fasting, studying and meditating on the Word of God, Praise and Worship, and yes, even journaling my dreams and visions and exercising, God started to move mightily in my life.

After several months of designing and selling t-shirts that displayed positive messages, I began thinking of the next item to add to my business resume. One day while on Facebook, I saw a simple, yet cute, blue bracelet. I contacted the individuals and they started designing jewelry for my company House of Stone by CoCo.

I served our Nation for twenty-one years (not including thirteen months in the U.S. Reserve)! I needed God now more than ever. As I shopped for another spiritual book to add to my collection, I heard Theology. I had a conversation with God and immediately enrolled into Liberty University.

After hearing from God, my husband and I stepped out on faith and started a Street and Outreach Ministry, New Beginnings International Outreach Ministries of Central Georgia (now Truth Revealed Global Ministries) located in Macon, Georgia. Our hearts are in serving, not to be served. Romans 8:28 (NKJV) *"And we know that all things work together for good to those who love God, to those who are the called according to His purpose."* Everything He has done in my life is positioning me in His Kingdom. Positioning me to do His will and His work. Every accomplishment is to do what He has already ordained would happen in my life. I didn't know then, but I now know, it was a part of His plan. My life due to Ministry would come full circle to where it all began as I started my journey nearly 25 years ago, in my hometown of Macon, Georgia.

The part-time jobs and military background prepared me for my business, House of Stone by CoCo, yet my strong faith, willingness to serve others and love for God prepared me for ministry. This is not the end. It's New Beginnings. To be continued….